But God Brought Me Through

By

Epathia Lockett

But God Brought Me Through

Acknowledgment

I would like to thank God for helping me write this book because if it wasn't for him, I would not be able to do this, and I would like to thank my husband and Joe Jr., and Bernard Lockett for pushing me on and most of all my pastor, William H. Walker Sr. He encourages me to go and to not give up, and I love him for that! And my New Bethlehem Baptist Church family!

But God Brought Me Through

"Prologue"

I was poor and I didn't have anything to eat. When I looked in the lunch room I saw other kids sitting down eating hot meals. At that moment, my eyes opened and I realized I was poor, but God brought me through!

Note: All scripture quotations are from the King James Version of the Bible!

But God Brought Me Through

Chapter One

When I was thirteen years old, my mother always would tell us to walk like a lady, sit like a lady, and most of all act like a lady. At a very young age she told me about boys. She said, "If you kiss a boy you will get pregnant!" and I believed her. I was so young, I didn't know any better. When I was in high school, this boy was the boy of my

But God Brought Me Through

life. I liked the way he walked, the way he talked, I liked the way his body was built, I loved that young boy. His name was Joe A. Lockett. I used to go home at night and just think about him. But back in the day, you couldn't just come to a boy and ask to go study with him. We were told a lady did not do anything like that. So, I began liking him from afar. Until one day I was at home and I wrote him a letter. We both rode the same bus and both got off at the same stop. I built up enough courage and gave him that letter I

But God Brought Me Through had written. Joe called me that same night. I was so happy to hear from him. My heart skipped a beat!

We were talking and he was running that line down to me; you know how boys do. He told me he has five girlfriends. I told him that I like him, but I'm not going to be number six. I told him I wanted to be the number one girlfriend.

My mother, Mrs. Magnolia King, she would always sit us down and tell us how to respect people's things. She told us not to

… But God Brought Me Through take anything that wasn't ours. When we got to the store, we'd better not take anything from that store. Mom loved us all. She was a mother of thirteen children, and she was trying her best to raise all of us right. I was small, I didn't know what my mother was going through. But God, he knows what my mother was going through. Mother used to line us all up every morning. We used to kneel down and pray to God. Mom used to go around the house singing songs to God and cleaning the house and praying.

But God Brought Me Through

When we were going to school we were poor. I used to wear my brother's pants under my dress to keep me warm. I did not have any gloves to wear. I used to wear socks on my hand to keep me warm. I didn't have but one pair of shoes, and that pair had hole in the bottom. So, I put cardboard in my shoes. When it rained, that cardboard got wet and made my socks wet, and I would walk all the way home from school. We couldn't do any better. But God, he knew my pain, and my hurt, and my shame. My

But God Brought Me Through

mother was making me apple better sandwiches for school. Mom didn't have any sandwich bags to put my sandwich in. So, she took my sandwich and used the bread wrapping to put my sandwich in. Before I got to school, the apple butter would leak out on the brown bag. I didn't want anyone to see that, so I threw away my lunch. I wouldn't have any lunch that day. I was beginning to see that I didn't have what other kids had. But I had a father that loved me. His name is Jesus.

But God Brought Me Through

"As the Father hath loved me, so have I loved you: continue ye in my love. If ye keep my commandments, ye shall abide in my love, even as I have kept my father's commandments, and abide in his love." (John 15:9-10 K.J.V.)

My mother used to cook beans every day and fatback. Every kind of beans and cornbread. She used to line us all up for our bowl of beans and cornbread. That's all we had and we thanked our God for our food. We did not have wood in the stove. My

But God Brought Me Through

brother used to walk the railroad tracks looking for wood or coal, or anything we could burn. We used to tear up Linoleum to put in the stove and break up wood chairs to keep warm. When we could not find anything, we used to all get in bed and put covers on us to keep us warm. The only time we had meat was on Sunday. One Sunday, it was chicken. The next Sunday, it was fish. We used to have grits with no butter. We used lard for butter. I had my hard times when I was small. We had powder milk to

But God Brought Me Through

drink when we were on low income. They let mom get this kind of food. They gave us spam meat, then they gave us cheese in a long brown box, and they gave us butter. We were so happy. We thought it was Christmas. We never had that much food at one time.

In our home, we did not have lights. We used kerosene lamps to see how to do our homework. I knew at a young age that God had a plan for me. At night, we used to all kneel down and pray. We went to church

But God Brought Me Through and Sunday school every Sunday. When we were talking and playing in church, all mom had to do was look back at us and we would straighten up. Mom wanted all her kids to know all about Jesus. It made me a better person and it made me act like the lady my mother wanted me to be. I met that boy, Joe A. Lockett one day. He saw me walking around at lunch time. He said, "How come you're not eating?" I told him I did not have any lunch money. Then he bought my lunch

But God Brought Me Through

for me. You see, God already made a way out of no way.

"Jesus answered and said unto them, ye do err, not knowing the scriptures, nor the power of God." (Matthew 22:29 K.J.V.)

Sometime in life you don't know which way to go, but there is a purpose in our life and God will lead us there. When trouble comes in our life, always remember God is there holding your hand. Time went on and he started calling me every day. We would talk on the phone for hours. My mom did

But God Brought Me Through

not say a word. I believed in my heart that God knew the beginning and the ending of my life. God – He didn't make any mistakes. One day, Joe and I were walking home from school, and He said, "I want to come over to your house and see you." But I had to ask my mom's permission before Joe could come over to the house. I went to my mother's room. I said, "Mom! Joe wants to come over to my house to see me." She said, "I don't know. I need to think about it."

But God Brought Me Through

Whenever he asked me again, I told him I would let him know. But mom knew how much I was in love with him. I told her I love him. She told me I didn't know what love is. I was young. I knew what was in my heart. And I knew he was the boy for me. I came home from school and she said yes, Joe can come over to the house.

I will never forget the day Joe came over one Sunday evening. I introduced him to my mother and sisters. Mom said she was going to give Joe and me a little privacy, so mom

But God Brought Me Through

closed the door. Every five minutes, mom came walking through the door. My mom had made about ten trips through that door looking. We kissed for a short time, and then one hour later mom called me into her room and told me Joe had to go home. We had to go to school the next day. Things were moving along nice. Joe would be looking for me in the morning at school.

"I pressed toward the mark for the prize of the high calling of God in Christ Jesus." (Philippians 3:14 K.J.V.)

But God Brought Me Through

This is what I call a mother's love for her children all the time. We didn't have any money to go to the doctor, so mom used to get a piece of cloth and put Xfinity in it, wrap it up, and put it around our neck. This was to keep us from getting a cold. Not only that, she used to give us turpentine and sugar in a spoon and give it to us to keep us from getting a cold. These were old home remedies. Back in the day, mom did all she could to keep us strong and well. Then she used to line all of us up and give us castor

But God Brought Me Through

oil and put a piece of peppermint in our mouth. As a child, I did not like this at all. I can tell you one thing; we never had a cold!

When my mom gave us them old home remedies, it didn't make any sense. All I can say is a mother knows what's best for her children all the time. My God gave my mother that gift to look out for her children. It's just like a bird. When the bird is small it stays in the nest. When the bird gets bigger, it leaves the nest and goes its own way. But the mother bird is somewhere watching over

But God Brought Me Through her baby. This is the way we should be about our children; watching over them and praying for them.

But God Brought Me Through

Chapter Two

We both were late getting on the school bus, all the school kids on the bus was standing up. But we had a seat on the bus, the same seat we always sat on. God changed everything in my life. I was happy and filled with joy because I was with the one I love. Joe had started coming over a lot

But God Brought Me Through

to the house. Now mom is beginning to like him. We did homework together. He stayed for dinner. We became very close.

One day I was getting off the bus, I missed a step and Joe caught me. If it wasn't for him I would have hurt myself. He is always looking out for me. Jesus is awesome. God, he is a great God. He is worthy of all the praise in my life. I know Joe is the boy I wanted in my life. He used to tell his mother, if I don't come home from school, I will be over at my girlfriend's

But God Brought Me Through

house. I like the respect he would give to me. Joe watches over me. He told me he loves me, now things are going so well.

We would hold hands together when I was going to my locker. Joe would be right there and when I open the locker door, Joe would kiss me before I went to class. This one boy in my study class (his name is Tod), would sit behind me every day and pull on my hair. I told Joe about Tod. He asked me how he looked, how tall he is, and I told him. A few days later, Tod stopped sitting

But God Brought Me Through where I was. He asked me how was study class. He asked me is that same boy pulling on my hair. I said, "No!" He said he told him to "leave you alone." I told him she is my girlfriend.

Joe didn't tell me anymore about the five girlfriends. So now I know that I am the only one, no other girl sat on the bus with Joe but me. It made me feel very special, and it made me love him that much more. In my life I have had good times and thank God for letting me be born.

But God Brought Me Through

"Then the word of the Lord came unto me, saying, Before I formed thee in the belly I knew thee; and before thou camest forth out of the womb I sanctified thee, and I ordained thee a prophet unto the nations." (Jeremiah, 1:4-5 K.J.V.)

Here comes a storm in my life I did not see coming. Mom told me we had to move. I couldn't believe it. Mom said she found a house in West End that she wanted to buy or rent. My brain was working very fast. Now this mean that I would not see Joe again,

But God Brought Me Through because we were going to move away. So, I told Joe about how we were going to move. He told me it was okay. He said it was alright, that I love you still. I will catch the bus to come and see you. When he said that, I knew he really cared about me.

We moved and I told him the day we were going to move. I told him I wasn't going to school that day. So, he took out too, to help us move in our house. Mom was asking Joe to move things here and there, until she got things the way she

But God Brought Me Through wanted them to be. Saturday, Joe came over to the house and mom told Joe that she needs a garage door. We had a garage with no door. That same day, Joe built that door onto the garage. He made a lock for the door so it could lock. We did not have a car, so mom put some boxes in the garage for storage. The sink needed to be fixed in the kitchen and bathroom and he fixed that for mom. He did not know he had a gift, but he did.

But God Brought Me Through

God gave us all a gift. You may have a gift for singing; that is the gift God gave to you; you may have a gift for giving people money to help them when hard times come their way; that may be your gift – if you look hard, God gave all of us a gift. So, ask God for your gift, He will give it to you.

Joe would leave Hayes High School and ride the bus to West End where I was. When I leave Parker High School and get home, Joe would be coming up the road to see me. I have learned there is nothing

But God Brought Me Through given to you in life to show us the right path to go. We are all His children. We might fall down, but we can get up. We have all sinned and fallen down, but God's grace and mercy can bring us through. I ask God to help me with this book. I did not write this book for any fame or fortune. I am writing this book for God to get the glory, and let you know that I cannot do anything without Jesus in my life. He has been with me all the way.

But God Brought Me Through
"For everyone that asketh receiveth; and he that seeketh findeth; and to him that knocketh it shall be opened."

(Matthew 7:8 K.J. V.)

I know when I pray, God hears me. I know he heard my cry. I am His child, I know He loves me, He Said in His word I will never leave you or forsake you. I will be with you always.

Parker High School was a new school for me. You see, I didn't know anyone. I felt so alone. But something said to me that

But God Brought Me Through

it was going to be alright. Just keep on pushing. That voice let me know it was Jesus talking, giving me comfort in my heart, comforting my mind, and my soul. I just love that soft touch he gives you just to let you know he cares.

Day by day, things started getting better. I started feeling better about myself. I became relaxed; I was not afraid anymore, because the Master of the ship had me in His hand. You got to get to know Jesus – who He is and what He is about. Jesus made me

But God Brought Me Through

strong. Jesus made me look to Him for help. There is someone out there right now who needs Jesus, but you don't know what to do. All you have to do is pray. Just talk to Him like I am talking to you right now and Jesus will hear you. He is a loving, kind God, and a God that really cares about you. He loves us all. As my pastor would say:

"Read your Bible and see what God is about. There is nothing too hard for my God. Your way may get dark, but my God can bring you through. Just trust Him."

But God Brought Me Through

Some people got jealous because Joe and I started showing our love. But then here comes another setback. Just when you think everything is going fine, here comes another one.

Miss Joeann came to my mother's house and told my mother that Joe was going with her daughter Helen for a year before he met me, and Miss Joeann told my boyfriend that he could start to see her daughter again. That made my mother mad, because all my mother could think about Joe was that he

But God Brought Me Through was trying to make a fool out of me. So, mom told me to tell Joe he could not come see me or call me again.

My heart was broken. It felt like my man was gone for good. All we had built to get there, and walking together, and holding hands – it was all gone now. But you see, I cry to the Lord. God saw my hurt, God saw my tears. God saw my broken heart. I know that my God was going to help me. I didn't give up. You see I know who I serve. His name is Jesus Christ, King of Kings. He

But God Brought Me Through is the only One that can change things for you.

"So, then faith cometh by hearing, and hearing by the word of God." (Romans 10:17 K.J.V)

And I had to believe in God's word, and know he will work this out for me.

But God Brought Me Through

Chapter Three

Joe came by my house and asked to talk to my mother. He told her he loved me, and when he met Helen it was a year before he met me and he did not know me then. He asked mom if he could start seeing me

But God Brought Me Through again. My mom said, "I will thank about it because I don't want my girl hurt by anyone." Days and weeks went by. My mom told me I could start back going with Joe. I told him my mother said it was alright for us to go back together. Every day he was away from me, my love got stronger and stronger. He said he loved me too.

When we moved to West End, mom bought a house there. We met our new neighbors, the Jacksons. Mr. and Mrs. Jackson had three daughters and two sons.

But God Brought Me Through

One was about my age and his name was John. Mom liked John for me. I did not like him because my heart was all for Joe. I did not pay any attention to John, but Mom would ask John over to the house when I got out of school. Joe hadn't gotten here yet, I asked mom please don't let John in the house, I don't like him. One day Joe was coming over to see me. Mom had asked John to come over to the house also. I did not know John was coming, but I knew Joe would be here soon. I didn't know what to

But God Brought Me Through

do and all of a sudden Joe came walking in and he asked who John was. Joe started staring at him and he asked him what he was here for. He let him know I was his girlfriend a little later John got up and left. I was so glad that was over with.

Now Joe is getting ready to go in the US Navy when he told me he signed up for four years. I cried because I knew this was another battle I would have to face without him in my life. He kept telling me how much he loved me. I was still crying, then

But God Brought Me Through

Joe said he wanted to marry me and ask mom for my hand in marriage. I was so happy! Joe came over to ask mom if he could marry me. He was going in the Navy soon and he wanted me to be his wife. Mom said yes, we could get married.

It was not a big church wedding; I did not have a white dress. His mother and Mom; we all went to the courthouse. We got married and it didn't matter to me about having a big wedding. Lots of people have big church weddings and receptions that

But God Brought Me Through

don't last long. That was not for us. All Joe wanted was to be together as husband and wife. We left the courthouse and went home to my mother's house. Mom had bought two white coconut cakes and drinks. We had hotdogs and that's all. We all were happy even if we didn't have any money. But God, he gave me the love of my life. Mom let us stay in her home when we got married. Joe was home for two weeks before he left for the Navy and again another set-back in my life; He told me to he had to

But God Brought Me Through
go, I started crying. He said he would be back as soon as his training was over. I have a husband going into the US Navy! Do you know I thanked God for being his wife and not his girlfriend anymore?

"The Lord is nigh unto them that are of a broken heart: and saveth such as be of a contrite spirit. Many are the afflictions of the righteous: but the Lord delivereth him out of them all." (Psalm 34: 18-19 K.J.V.)

The Lord is close to the broken and saves those who are crushed in spirit. The

But God Brought Me Through

righteous person may have many troubles, but the Lord delivers him from them all.

At that time, I prayed I know God heard my prayer. All of a sudden, I stopped crying and felt a lot better. I don't know how I would have made it, but God controlled my path and he directs me every day. Joe was gone but I could write him a letter every day telling him how much I love him and how I missed being in his arms. Joe wrote back telling me how busy he was. He said he can write me at night. One day he wrote me

But God Brought Me Through

asking why I was not writing him. I wrote back and told him I was writing every day. One day during mail call Joe said he got five letters at one time. Days and months passed and I asked him when he is coming home. He said he didn't know. Day after day I prayed for him that God would bring Joe through.

"Call to me and I will answer you, and tell you great and unsearchable things you do not know." (Jeremiah 33:3 K.J.V)

But God Brought Me Through

I was so young when I got married to Joe, but one thing I can say I know Jesus Christ, because of my mother taking us to church and Sunday school. Mom had us kneel down before God and pray at a young age. Jesus Christ knows me, Jesus knows my voice because I had a personal relationship with God when I was young. That's why it's very important for you to know God for yourself. God knew my name, he knew my voice. I will tell anyone, have your own personal relationship with

But God Brought Me Through God. When you pray, be real and God will hear you. Jesus is looking at your heart, Jesus already knows what you need before you ask him. When you ask, believe in your heart that God will give it to you.

"Ye lust, and have not: ye kill and desire to have, and cannot obtain: ye fight and war, yet ye have not, because ye ask not. Ye ask, and receive not because ye ask amiss, that ye may consume it upon your lust."

(James 4:2-3 K.J.V.)

But God Brought Me Through

James tells us that all our fighting and coveting is ridiculous. The reason you have not is because you ask not. I prayed and asked God to send Joe home to me. He wrote me a letter and said he is coming home from boot camp. He told me the day and time to meet him at the airport. We got home and he said he would be with me for two weeks. I was so happy! I had my husband back home with me again! Every hour of the day we were together. It meant so much to me. Joe was telling me about the

But God Brought Me Through work he had to do in boot camp to pass.

Mom knew how sad I was when Joe was not there. She was glad we were together. Joe said the Navy will separate the men from the boys. He said his whole outlook on life changed. We had a lot of making up to do.

But God Brought Me Through

Chapter Four

I felt so safe with him when I was in his arms. I don't want him to let me go. All the way home he was kissing me. He just couldn't keep his hands off of me! I told

But God Brought Me Through

him, "baby, let's wait till we get home!" He kept saying how much he missed me. He said I love you so much and I didn't know how much I missed you until you were away from me. Time could not come fast enough for him. Now love was in the air.

The two weeks went by so fast, and now it's time for him to leave me again. Now I am facing sadness all over again. This was the best two weeks I've ever had. With my husband, his order was taking him to Davis Ville, Rhode Island for school. He said he

But God Brought Me Through

was going to be gone for six weeks for training on the base. I took him to the airport. Here I am trying to be a brave wife. He told me I need to get used to him leaving me because he will be coming home for a short while and then he will leave. He said he was trying to make this better for both of us, and one day I'll see how much God will bless us to make it better for us. I know he is right but that didn't make it any better for me to see the man I love walk out. For me it hurt and I felt a lot of pain in my heart. He

But God Brought Me Through had a job to do in the Navy and I had to understand this as his wife.

Time passed on, and I prayed to God to give me strength as his wife. I would write Joe all the time. He wrote me when he could and in one of his letters he said "I have a lot of studying to do to pass the test." This was the longest six weeks of my life time.

Joe called and told me he was coming home. He told me what day and time he wanted me at the airport. When I saw his

But God Brought Me Through

face, I was so happy. You just wouldn't believe how overcome with joy I was! One more time I will have my husband. We will be a family again. But God heard my prayers, when he got home he was telling me his new order and where he was going this time. He said he was going to Gulfport, Mississippi. I said okay, my main aim was not on where he was going. I was glad he was home for two weeks and you better believe we made the best of it. I was just

But God Brought Me Through

looking at him so hard. I told him I just want to remember him when he goes back.

Two weeks come to an end, only a woman can understand when your man is going away and you know that it's going to be a long time before you see him. From a woman's point of view that's hard for her to take. You see she is looking at the big picture, she is alone; her man is miles and miles away. That's your husband and you can't hold him when you want to, or kiss him when you want to. That's where the

But God Brought Me Through

pain comes in, because you love him.

That's what makes you cry. You cry for him. When Joe left this time, I was trying to be brave. I held back the tears. Now time passed, weeks passed. I started to get sick. I couldn't keep anything on my stomach. When I tried to eat anything or any kind of food I would throw up. All I could do was to lie down for a while. Mom said Pat, you need to go to the doctor and find what's wrong with you. So, I went. They ran some tests and then the doctor called me the next

But God Brought Me Through

day and told me I was pregnant. He set me up with an appointment. I told my mother and she said not to tell Joe till he comes home. My mother was happy for me. A few weeks later Joe called, and said he was coming home. When he got home, I told him I told him I was pregnant with his child. Joe's eyes got so big, he was so happy. He started saying we needed to move and get a bigger place. So, we started looking for an apartment.

But God Brought Me Through

"But my God shall supply all you need according to his riches in glory by Christ Jesus." (Philippians 4:19 K.J.V)

I am facing another struggle in my life. I have a baby, and a husband in the Navy. He can leave me at any time. I know all my tests I have in my life. They come to make me strong.

"I can do all things through Christ which strengtheneth me." (Philippians 4:13 K.J.V.)

It is Christ in me that helps me to make it.

But God Brought Me Through

So, I say let the setbacks come. My God can do anything. He just can't fail. We moved into an apartment in Loveman Village. This is a new stage in our life. This is my first time to take up housekeeping. I am still having morning sickness. I went to the doctor and he gave me some iron pills to take every day. My body was changing. I cannot wear my clothes so we went to the mall to buy some outfits. I was so glad Joe was going to be a father. Now he was talking about a bigger

But God Brought Me Through

place! Here we are, we need furniture. So, we bought two-bedroom sets, a sofa, chair, and a table to go in the kitchen. Now I feel like the woman that God has made me to be. A mother and a wife.

"As for me, I will call upon God; and the Lord Shall save me." (Psalm 55:16 K.J.V.)

The months started going by and now it's time to have my baby. I will never forget. Joe was still in the Navy when I had the baby. It was a boy and he was seven pounds, 14 ounces. When I woke up they

But God Brought Me Through had put me in a suite. That evening the nurse brought my baby to me. He was so small I didn't know how to hold him. She was nice and showed me how to hold his head up at all times. Joe came to the hospital to see me and our baby. He said the same thing, I told him to hold his head up close to your body and hold him lightly.

Now the time passed and it was almost time for him to go back so he took us home and the next day he told me he was thinking about getting out of the Navy because I'll

But God Brought Me Through

need help. His time was almost up, I was so glad God heard my prayer. You see all you have to do is stand on God's word and he will bring you through every time. All the lonely nights without my husband, all the tears I shed, but I knew in my mind God was going to make it someway, somehow. He was going to fix it for me and I believe that. I held on to that hope.

Now Joe is out of the Navy and he is looking for a job. He left early in the morning and went looking for a job but he

But God Brought Me Through

couldn't find anything. He called me at noon and said he looked everywhere and couldn't find anything. So, he went out the next day and we prayed together that God will help him find a job. He called and told me he found a job. He said he went to the manager at Britling Cafeteria downtown. The manager told him to try Highland Avenue. They were hiring up there. He got the job! He was so happy he had family and a job.

But God Brought Me Through

Joe became a waiter. The manager gave him a red jacket. This is the beginning of a new field for him. At first it was a struggle trying to be a good husband, looking for a job but God helped him find one. Joe didn't care, he wanted to work. We are a real family now! I had to get used to the baby and caring for him. Also trying to be the best wife, but God brought us through. We are both in the real world now! It was a big change for both of us. As the month was passing, we lived in Loveman Village for

But God Brought Me Through nine months. One day we got a letter saying they were going to raise our rent. Joe said to me he was not going to pay this! He said for a few dollars more we can get a home. So that is what God helped us to do. This is bigger and Joe Jr. loved the backyard. Now Joe Jr. is three. God blessed us with another, blessing Bernard. Now our family is complete.

"Therefore whosoever heareth these sayings of mine, and doeth them, I will liken

But God Brought Me Through

him unto a wise man, which built his house upon a rock." (Matthew 7:24 K.J.V.)

This was our wise decision. Troubles come again. My husband got sick and I was not working at the time. Things got hard for a while but God took care of him. We kept the faith that God will make him better, and God did take care of him.

But God Brought Me Through

Chapter Five

Sometimes we do not know which way

Jesus wants us to go, and I will tell anyone

But God Brought Me Through

try to get closer to Jesus. Because you do not know when you will need him.

Things started changing for me. The kids are getting older now. I put Joe Jr. in school and Bernard in preschool, and I went looking for a job. And I found a job at St. Vincent's Hospital. Only Jesus open that window for me. Now I can help Joe out and we can work together on what we need to do for our future.

I call my mom every day checking up on her, to make sure she was alright. One day I

But God Brought Me Through

called her, she told me she was sick. I told her when I get off from work I would come over. I went to Mom's house and she was lying down. But when I came in she sat up in the chair. I said Mom, do you want me to take you to the doctor and she said no. She told me she was alright now that I was here. I feel a little better. Mom smiled and we talked about everything. She called in both my sisters and she was smiling big.

When I saw that Mama was alright, I told her I had to go home and pick the kids

But God Brought Me Through

up and cook, and she told me she didn't want me to leave. She said call Joe, tell him to pick up the kids and you can cook later. So, I did what Mama said. Mama kept on telling me how much she loves me and I said, "Mama, I love you too." So, she came over and hug me, it was so tight and she kissed me. At that time, I did not know this will be my last time I would see my mother alive.

I stayed with Mama all that evening until night came. I said Mom, I really got to go.

But God Brought Me Through

She said okay. She understood. So, when I was leaving out the door, Mama grabbed me again. She hugged me and kissed me again. I said Mom; I want some of your flower in this pot. She gave me the whole pot. She said you can have it. Then I left and went home.

I called Mama the next day but the phone kept on ringing. I called on my lunch break, but the phone kept ringing. I called my sister. I told her I can't get Mama. I told her to call Mama and see will she pick

But God Brought Me Through

up the phone. My sister called and said Pat, you need to come to Mama's house. We can't get in.

We called the police. She said they were on their way. I told my manager about everything. She said go home, it's alright. When I got there, Yvonne and Euphoria was there outside. Five minutes later the police came. There were two police officers, male and female. They went around the back and the side of the house. The police broke the door in and told us to stay outside. They would let us know when we can come in. The female officer came to us and said that Mama had passed and it was alright for us to come in. Yvonne started crying and Euphoria started crying too. We found my Mama on the floor. She had her mouth open. Yvonne started screaming and she was holding Mama. Euphoria was crying and said Mama was cold. She got cover to cover Mama up. And as for me, all I could do was cry; I was with Mama the day before.

But God Brought Me Through

The lady officer told all of us we had to leave. She called the coroner to pick up Mama's body. When they came to take Mama away, we were all still crying. We locked up the house and left. The next day I called my manager and told her my Mama had passed. She told me to take all the time I need.

I still don't know why God let me spend the last day with my Mama. Out of thirteen children, God chose me. That very day, I

But God Brought Me Through knew then that God chose me to be with my Mama. And I thank him every day for that.

We got together to check on Mama's policy. When we got to the funeral home, the man told all of us how much it would take to bury Mom. He looked at the policy and told us we did not have enough money to bury Mama. Now here comes another storm in all our family life. We all called the sister and brother from Washington, D.C., sister from New York, and sister and brother from Texas.

But God Brought Me Through

My husband told the funeral home man we would get the money for my Mama. The funeral home man told my husband, "Son, do you know what you are doing? You are just the son-in-law." All my brothers and sisters came down. My husband had a meeting with them. He told all of them how much money we need. So, we all got together and it was done. I will tell anybody please check your mother and father policy, because my mother just knew she had enough money to be buried.

But God Brought Me Through

We had the funeral and everyone was screaming and crying, but me – all I could think about was the last day I spent with Mama and how I knew how happy Mama was. How she was smiling when I looked at her. That is what comforted me. That's how I made it through.

The funeral was over everyone was over Mama's house. Telling about the good old days, but one thing I found out that my mother had called all her children before she

But God Brought Me Through

died. They told me they wish they were with Mama the day before she died.

I still don't know what God have for me, but one thing I do know: whatever he wants me to do, I will do. Because I know that I am His child. Time went on but things were not the same without Mama. You could tell Mom anything and you would not hear it again. I really missed my Mom. Then I started to read my Bible all about Jesus. I had to learn about Him. I pray every day asking God to take the pain away. For the

But God Brought Me Through

loss of my mother, days and months pass and the pain was still with me. A year passed and I was still thinking about Mama. All I could do was pray. I kept on praying to Jesus, He was the only one who could take my hurt away. That's when I made Jesus my Father because I knew he would always be by my side. Because His Word said, let your conversation be without covetousness, and be content with such things as ye have. For he hath said I will never leave thee nor forsake thee.

But God Brought Me Through
Hebrew 13:5 (K.J.V.)

Chapter Six

But God Brought Me Through

As time progressed, Joe said Pat, I'm looking for a better job for the family. The kids are getting bigger now and they need more. Joe found a job at U.S. Pipe. It was a good job, but it was a night shift. But he wanted to take the job. This was good at first, but a night shift job was going to pull him away from the boys and me. That meant I was going to be the with boys a lot more than he was. One day I set the boys down and told them that Daddy was

But God Brought Me Through

working hard to help keep what we have. I also told them that we both love them, but bills had to get paid.

I was working in the morning and getting them ready for school. Coming home from work, I was tired. But I had to keep on pushing. I had to cook dinner, make sure the boys ate dinner, get them ready for bed, and help them with their homework. It was so much for me until I had started laying the boys' clothes out at night so all they had to do was get ready.

But God Brought Me Through

Then I would be getting ready for work. I had to go to the PTA meeting to check on how they were doing in class.

When they were in any programs, the boys wanted me to be there. I was always there for them. When they were in plays in school, I was there. Then I found out it is more than being a mother. You also have to act the role of a mother. Talk to your sons. Tell them you are with them because they need you. Let them know that you love them. Tell your child how proud you are of

But God Brought Me Through them. I would never forget Joe Jr.'s grades were failing. His daddy told him he had to bring his grades up. Jr. started studying and doing his homework. Joe Jr. would get up at 3 o'clock in the morning and study for his test he had to take that day. When he gets home, Joe Jr. would have made an 'A' on the test. We both try to be good parents to the boys. On Saturdays, when Joe was off, that was his time with the boys. He showed them how to play football. Joe bought them a basketball goal and they would all play.

But God Brought Me Through

Joe bought the boys both baseball gloves and play with them. One day Joe was showing the boys how to be a big boy and take care of themselves when other kids pick on them.

When Joe had time, he would set them down and tell the boys how to be a real man. It is so good to have a father to take time out for you, and to talk to you. A boy needs to know certain things to help him to become a man. And same as a girl, she needs her mother to help her to become a real woman.

But God Brought Me Through

Girls need their mother to lead them and guide them. But out of all you tell them, you need to tell them most of all they need to know Jesus Christ. When you are in trouble, Jesus will be there for you. Can't nobody do you like Jesus, and he is also a Comforter. When you can't sleep, he sends his angel to hold you and to put you to sleep. I am telling you about this because I know you see. I try him one day and he turned my whole life around. That is why I love Him so much.

But God Brought Me Through
But God change things around for me.

When I look back over my life, how young I was and how God showed me a boy that I fell in love with? Now he is a man, and a father. I thank God for letting me meet him because God worked through him and blessed us with these things. I never thought I would ever have a man like Joe. God is a good God, and that's why I praise His name. I will tell all of you, get to know Jesus because we don't know what life will bring us. And Baby, I am a witness. He brought

But God Brought Me Through me out without a doubt; I know what he is still doing for me.

Look at your life. Take a ten-minute checklist; write down on a piece of paper what you need to change in your life to make it better. Then write down on a piece of paper where you are now. Then ask yourself, am I happy without God in my life. Are you happy with God in your life? You decide if it had not been for God on my side. I don't know how I would have made it. Don't take it lightly.

But God Brought Me Through
"And it shall come to pass, that before they call, I will answer; and while they are yet speaking, I will hear." (Isaiah 65:24 K.J.V)

Joe and I have changed because we have Jesus in our life. We taught our sons about Jesus. They both know in time of need, Jesus is there for them in their life. Joe Jr. and Bernard Lockett are grown men who know they are starting on their life for themselves. I just hope they don't forget about Jesus Christ. We all make mistakes,

But God Brought Me Through

but God, He is always there to help you clean it up. We may fall down, but we can get up, Jesus will bring us where we need to be. Mrs. Martha Lockett came over to our house and had dinner with us. We were back together, one big happy family. Now Joe Jr. is grown up. He told his father he didn't want to work for anyone, so Joe Jr. went to the Navy. When Joe Jr. got out of the Navy he told his father he had his mind made up. He had a goal; he didn't want to take any more orders so he didn't.

But God Brought Me Through

Chapter Seven

But God Brought Me Through

He started selling houses and when that didn't work out, he went to the radio station. Joe Jr. came over one day and told his father and I that he wanted to be on the radio. You see, everybody can't see your dream, and your goal because God didn't give that dream to everyone. As a mother, I knew that was what Joe Jr. wanted. I could see the drive in his eyes. Every mother knows their son. This is what he wants to do. Joe Jr. went on with God's help and he made it!

But God Brought Me Through

Not only on radio, but he has his own TV show on Monday nights. You see God gave him his dream. When God gives you a dream, don't just sit there and say I can't do this. Yes, you can! Remember you can do all things through Christ!

"Salute every saint in Christ Jesus. The brethren which are with me greet you." (Philippians 4:21 K.J.V.)

Bernard gets grown and decided to leave Birmingham and he went to live in Lafayette, Louisiana. He bought a home

But God Brought Me Through and got a good job offshore for Shell.

Bernard remembers his teaching about Jesus Christ so he joined a church. The name of the church is: Good Hope Baptist Church. Reverend Ricky E. Carter. Bernard has a daughter; her name is Briana. She is going to Troy University. Bernard has been a member of his church for ten years and he loves his Pastor. To me it is so funny how you have two sons and you would think they would have way's alike but they are so different as day and night. This is the way

But God Brought Me Through

God had the second seed turn out. I am a true believer that, when you live for God and only him, he will give you your heart's desire. Joe Sr. and I work hard to give our sons what they need. When they were young our sons had new shoes. We both gave them everything they wanted. But you see we both were poor. Joe Sr. and I wanted our sons to have the things we didn't have when we were coming up.

"Be careful for nothing; but in everything by prayer and supplication with

But God Brought Me Through

thanksgiving let your requests be made known unto God." (Philippians 4:6 K.J.V)

One day I was at the clinic with my baby and a lady was sitting next to me. We started talking and she asked to see my baby. She told me how pretty he was, and I told her I will be so glad when he gets big. The old lady said, when you they are small, you are carrying them in your arms, and you can protect them, but when they grow up you are carrying them in your heart. At the time, I did not understand what she meant. But

But God Brought Me Through now I am older, I really see what she was trying to tell me.

Because I carry them in my heart, I am asking God to take care of them. And I am praying for God to watch over them, so now I got it. God and his angel are helping me to carry them. Thank God for Jesus. I thank him every day.

All of my setbacks and disappointments, Jesus brought me through. So, don't sit there crying saying I don't know what to do. I don't know which way to go. Call on Jesus

But God Brought Me Through
Christ the great I am, The King of Kings, the beginning and ending, the Lord of Lords, Alpha and Omega, when I think about his goodness and all he has done for me, my soul cries out, thank you Lord Jesus for blessing me, it's a blessing serving God. He brought me this far and I know he will take me on. My Pastor would say you are all going to get this stuff, in all my appointed time. I have depended on him to help me through my disappointment and all my trials and tribulations. It was Jesus that made me

But God Brought Me Through strong. He gave me strength. He made me be the strong woman that I am today. I give him all my thanks, all honor, and all praise goes to my God because I know who I am in Jesus Christ and I know he loves me!

God helped us to buy a house for sale. I told Joe something just wasn't right, we needed to give God thanks for all the blessings and everything he had done for us. So, we started going to a church in Forestdale, the name of the church is True Life Missionary Baptist Church. We kept

But God Brought Me Through

on going to the church, we came to pray, meeting and Bible study, and Sunday school. We really like the church! So, one day Reverend Steve Small Jr. was talking to us, we really began to fit in; the pastor calls us both to his office and said "Mr. Lockett, I'm thinking about making you and sister Lockett Deacon of the church."

We stayed in our home in Forestdale for 19 years. Joe Sr. came home one day and said honey I want to talk to you about something that's been on my mind. For a

But God Brought Me Through

while we sat down and he said that he wants us to move and buy a retirement home for us. I said honey are you sure about this? You better really think about this. The boys are gone now and we decided to think about it. Time went on; he came back, and said I'm not going to move until God tells me to move!

But God Brought Me Through

Chapter Eight

One day Joe was at work and he heard a voice say now is the time. When Joe got

But God Brought Me Through
home, he told me about it and I said okay.
I'm telling everyone this. You got to know
his voice and Jesus said my sheep know my
voice.

"My sheep hear my voice, and I know
them, and they follow me." (John 10-27
(K.J.V.)

We put the house up for sale and sold it
in two weeks. You got to listen for God's
voice. I told him he needed to think because
I didn't want to do anything that is not in the
will of God. I asked God, Lord it's not my

But God Brought Me Through

will, but Lord let your will be done. I just want you to know the real estate man said you don't need to start looking for a house now, because it hasn't been on the market that long. I'm not boasting or anything like that, but when God moves, he moves. My God is a passed over Lamb. He died for all of our sins. Because He lives I can face tomorrow.

I don't know about you, but my mind is made up. Jesus is My Everything. He is my mother and Jesus are my father. He is my

But God Brought Me Through hope for tomorrow; I am sold out for Jesus Christ. For Christ, the solid rock I stand. All other ground is sinking sand; we all must stand on the Rock. That Rock is Jesus, we go through our ups and downs, our sad times, our happy times but that life we must face this all head-on because we have someone right by our side. God sees every one of us the same.

"Confess your faults one to another, and pray one for another, that ye may be healed.

But God Brought Me Through

The effectual fervent prayer of a righteous man availeth much." (James 5:16 K.J.V.)

We all come to the crossroads in life, but Jesus can tell you the right road to take. Don't say I don't know what I need to do, just go forward and Jesus will lead you to the right road. One road maybe dark. That's not the right road. Then the other road may have a shining light that's , Jesus Christ's Road. He is the light of the world, he brings us light.

But God Brought Me Through

We were looking for a house because we didn't have anywhere to go. We put the furniture in storage so Joe and I pray that God will show us the right way. The thing about life is it's not always easy. You don't have it in your head all the time. But remember God is able to carry you through. I tried him one day and my password says don't you ever give up on God because He is able. You see, God, He cannot lie, He is a true God to his word. Some people may lie

But God Brought Me Through to you, but God he is not like people. He is there to see you through.

"For his anger endureth but a moment; in his favour is life: weeping may endure for a night, but joy cometh in the morning." (Psalm 30:5 K.J.V.)

Jesus brings you Joy. Just go on and endure that hurt, but there is a bright side somewhere. So, when I got off from work Joe picked me up and we went looking for a house. They were building some houses. They had them for sale so we came in and

But God Brought Me Through

looked around. In one house we didn't know the salesman was inside. We went to the back looking at the yard and deck, and then the man came out on the deck and said you can see a whole lot better if you come in. He showed us around and Joe asked him if they hold houses for people. He said no, first come first serve. We said okay, but God knows what we need, when you looking for anything put God in it. Pray about it, man does not have the last say so, if you are a child of the most-high King he

But God Brought Me Through

will give you what you need. When we didn't have a house, God saw our need in everything you got to believe in him, and know that he will bring you through. All we said is okay, God let everything go through all right. When we got the house, we thanked God for his Blessing. So now we need to worship him. I'm not bragging, when you want God to bless you, he will bless you. By praying you get close to him, take one day at a time and read your Bible.

But God Brought Me Through

Start with something small, and read it over and over again until it gets in your spirit. Then ask God to give you wisdom to understand. The next day read a little more, you see you're putting Jesus in your life every day, Jesus Word is powerful. Jesus' Word is Everlasting, His word will start working on you. God loves us all; He holds all of us in his arms. Jesus is not short of His Word, and God does not lie. God has blessed us but something was missing. We need to find a church home. We went to a

But God Brought Me Through

lot of churches but God was not there. Some churches were cold and they weren't telling people about Jesus Christ. So, one day we heard about New Bethlehem Baptist Church on the radio, and I told Joe I want to see that man. I like the way he was talking about Jesus, so we went there on Sunday. The Pastor's name is William H. Walker Senior. When we came in the door, the greeters were so nice. When we walked in, I thought I was walking in heaven. I felt the spirit of the Lord all around my head and

But God Brought Me Through

feet. The lady took us right down front of the church. I was trying to hold it back, because we were new visitors. I just wanted to hear God's word that day, we got home and Joe asked me how I liked that church. I told him this is the one, then we started going. Pastor just started preaching and it looks like something on the inside started working on me. And every time the Pastor would jump up, you can feel his power and his Spirit just falling. Pastor would always hold his Bible in his hand. One thing I like

But God Brought Me Through about my Pastor is he comes right from the Bible to let you see for yourself. He doesn't make anything up. I will call him my Bible word preacher, that's why I love him. The spirit so high I want to take out running but I have to hold myself because we are still new. And that was so hard for me. One Sunday Mr. Lockett and I joined the church and that was when it all began. I got all my learning and teaching at New Bethlehem Baptist Church. We went to Sunday school and Bible study.

But God Brought Me Through

"Now unto him that is able to do exceeding abundantly above all that we ask or think, according to the power that worketh in us."

(Ephesians 3:20(K.J.V.)

Chapter Nine

But God Brought Me Through
Now this is our complete circle: Jesus

led us to the right church, a Jesus church.

It's so funny when you are happy and you

looking toward Jesus, something always

come trying to bring you down. Now there

comes my struggle in the year 2013. Joe Sr.

got sick. God been keeping him all this

time, but in everyone's life rain will fall and

test your faith. But I was there right by his

side, and Jesus was with us every step of the

way. My Pastor came over to see Joe and

pray for us and wish him well. Then people

But God Brought Me Through from the Sunday school class came over to see him and brought him a card. You just don't know how much that meant to us. He cares just that much about us, it made my heart full. You see, God looks beyond my faults and saw our needs. Jesus was there in all my tribulation. Jesus found compassion for me, and today I love Him so much. For He look on the inside of us and saw our heart. No one can do this but Jesus – nobody. You can look high, but nobody can do this but Jesus.

But God Brought Me Through

"Jesus Christ is the same yesterday, and today, and forever." (Hebrew 13:8 K.J.V.)

We did not get behind on our bills. We didn't have to worry about the house note. We didn't have to worry about food, we had it. I want you to see what God did for us, and I'm not taking this lightly. I just want you to know: God had a plan for us, and he took care of us. God will take care of us all, but you got to believe that. He is God and He just can't fail you. If you believe in Him, He is the head of our life, and he is the

But God Brought Me Through Beginning of our life. He already knows how each and everyone's life is going to turn out. Remember He is God, He don't need no help. Just trust Him, have our hope and faith in Him, and He will never fail. We are looking at everything (but God). We looking at people and how they talking about you, look for God. He is the Author and Finisher of our faith.

"What shall we then say to these things? If God be for us, who can be against us?" (Romans 8:31 K.J.V.)

But God Brought Me Through
Jesus Christ is the same yesterday today and forever: Jesus don't change. We may change but Jesus, He is always the same. Sometimes we have to look to Jesus, who for the joy that was set before him endured the cross.

"Looking unto Jesus the author and finisher of our faith; who for the joy that was set before him endured the cross, despising the shame, and is set down at the right hand of the throne of God." (Hebrews 12:2 K.J.V.)

But God Brought Me Through

You see, Jesus, He died on the cross for you and for me, and for all of us. And He never said a word. This is how much he loves us, He could have had a whole legion of angels come and get him down off the cross. But Jesus had a mission to do. He wanted to do what His Father told him to do. That is why when you call on Jesus Christ, something happens. The earth shake, the wind blows, and the name of Jesus; just His name is highly exalted. Because when you call him, He will hear you and then things

But God Brought Me Through

start happening good for you. When you follow Jesus, you will suffer. People may not like you because you following Jesus. People may talk bad things about you when you follow Jesus. But that's alright. God got a plan, and it will work out for our good. Take out sometime now – look back over your life. I know he protects you from something. All you have to do is thank Him for what He has done for you.

Mr. Lockett decided to join the male choir. He really like singing in the choir.

But God Brought Me Through

He made some friends, and in his Sunday school class, he was well on his way. You can see the happiness; there is something about God's grace and mercy: His loving and kindness and compassion. And God brought Joe out alright. That's why I say when you call on Jesus, everything good start happening. I feel something started working down on the inside.

Now we have seasons; the four seasons, spring, summer, autumn, winter. In everyone's life, we all have a season. Your

But God Brought Me Through season maybe spring, we don't know what the Lord is going to take us through. You may have a really good job, but one day the boss calls you in and say your job is gone. This is your season. How can your bill be paid? How can your rent be paid? Jesus, He will go down with you in your season, and He will bring you through. He already has a plan for you. But believe in Him, because He cares for you. When bad seasons come in your life, the Lord hears your cry and your tears.

But God Brought Me Through
"For his anger endureth but a moment; in his favour is life: weeping may endure for a night, but joy cometh in the morning." (Psalm 30:5 K.J.V.)

Jesus is your joy: if you trust Him, He will bring you out.

Here is a list of seasons that come in life; pain, disappointment, discourage, lack of faith, lack of belief, lack of trust, lack of happiness, and lack of joy. I want you to know God got it all in control. In God

But God Brought Me Through appointed time, God and only God can get you out of your season.

Chapter Ten

But God Brought Me Through

I decided to join the choir at New Bethlehem Baptist Church. When I join, I didn't know anyone there. I got put in the alto area. We had a rehearsal every Thursday. The choir was so big, but the Lord helped me to fit right in. I love all the songs we sing. Whatever I do for God, I would always take it seriously. One day, I was walking in the life center, and I met Mrs. Edna Walker. She is the first lady of our church. We started talking and she asked me would I like to come to the

But God Brought Me Through mission. She said, just sit in on the class and see how I like it. So, I went to the mission class. I enjoyed the teaching. I kept on going. You see, the mission would go to the nursing home. Someday we would go to the really sick people at home and we would pray for them and sing them a song. And our teacher would teach the Word of God. This is how we helped the sick get the Word of God, and our Pastor would come by and pray for them. We made up baskets for people that could not get out.

But God Brought Me Through

In our church, we are all one big happy family. And I believe that they all were my mission family. Time is moving on and we are still at New Bethlehem Baptist Church. I have got all of my teaching and learning here with Pastor Walker. It's like he charged up my battery. When I come to church, I don't come to see what Mary is wearing or see what color hat Mary is wearing. I come to worship a true and living God, and that is all that matter to me. If the Spirit hit me, the shoes may go one way and

But God Brought Me Through

the hat may go another way, but I don't care. My God is using me. I can't sit like a wooden Indian, and like God have never done anything for me. My Pastor would say on Sunday, "How many of you thank God for waking you up in the morning?" He says don't take that lightly, because he could pass by your house and you would be still sleeping. So, you better thank him while you can.

Joe and I started going more to Sunday school. I have learned you can't get all your

But God Brought Me Through learning when your Pastor preaches on Sunday. You get your learning in Bible study. There you will get your learning in. Since I started going to Bible study, I have learned so much about Jesus Christ. I take notes and I go back home and read my Bible. You got to know about Jesus Christ! Our Bible study teacher Rev. Jessie Vann let us do five-minute messages about what we learned at the end of every chapter. And he gives us homework. When I first came to the class, I didn't know whether or not I

But God Brought Me Through
could fit in so I started praying asking God
to help me understand. You see, when you
make one step to God, He will make two to
you. But one thing I can say, He told me
just keep on coming, Sister Lockett. You
will get there.

Pastor Vann always ask do you
understand, and if you don't he will break it
down so good, even a child can understand.
So, this is how I got my teaching. We came
every Wednesday, but I couldn't wait
because I was hungry for God's Word. I

But God Brought Me Through

come home sharing what I learned to Joe and call my sons telling them what we did in Bible study. God is changing my life. Since I met Jesus, He let me know He is there for me. When I can't sleep, He always comforts me. I am so glad I know him. You know, God is real. God talks to me, He tells me I am His own. God will talk to you, just try Him. Get down on our knees and just talk to him. Take out a little time and spend with Him.

But God Brought Me Through

And one thing I like about God, you can talk to him about anything and you won't hear it again. Now you see why I say," He is my everything." He gives you food when you don't have any; all I can say you better try Him. He is a God that will stick closer than a brother.

There are times in my life I had to depend on God. The year 2014, my struggle came. I was having foot pain in my instep. I went to the doctor and she told me I had to have an operation on my foot. I told my

But God Brought Me Through

husband what the doctor said. He said, "Pat, I think you should do it. You've been hurting for a while." My doctor told me I would be on crutches for a good while. So, I had surgery. Joe Sr. was right by my side. I came home on crutches. Joe helped me out, but the next day Joe had to go to work and I was home all alone on crutches. I didn't have lunch because I couldn't open the icebox good with the crutches, and I could not put my foot on the floor. Now when Joe gets off from work he would always bring

But God Brought Me Through

me dinner. So, I just prayed out to God.

Now you see what I mean. I had to depend

on God. I would read God's Word, pray,

and go on. You see, this was my season,

and I had to go through. I could not say

Lord, why you doing this to me? Sometime

you have to take the bitter with the sweet

and pray to God. We all have our test in our

life, but you can't lay blame on anyone else

to come and make you strong. But you

know what, I thank God that I was still

alive. You need to thank Him for small

But God Brought Me Through things and when you thank Him, thank Him form your heart.

Things were progressing. I started feeling better and I could use my crutches a lot better and I could do for myself. Now you see how God brought me out. That is why I thank Him every day, because He is worthy of all the honor, glory and praise. I got a right to praise Him, because He is my best friend.

This is my testimony. As I was writing this book, Satan got me down. My left knee

But God Brought Me Through

went out on me. It was hurting so bad I had to go to my doctor. My doctor thought I had a blood clot in my leg. I went Friday for a test and they didn't find anything. If God be for you, who can be against you?

"What shall we then say to these things? If God be for us, who can be against us?" (Romans 8:31 K.J.V.)

But God brought me through.

"So, do not fear, for I am with you always." (Isaiah 41:10 K.J.V.)

But God Brought Me Through

www.ingramcontent.com/pod-product-compliance
Lightning Source LLC
Chambersburg PA
CBHW032052150426
43194CB00006B/508